To, my d[...]

Gro[...]

Never give up

reaching for the

sky

Deb

(& the boys)

REACHING FOR STARS

✳ ✳ ✳ ✳

reflections on a journey
through life and living

JANINE SHEPHERD

RANDOM HOUSE
AUSTRALIA

Random House Australia Pty Ltd
20 Alfred Street, Milsons Point, NSW 2061
http://www.randomhouse.com.au

Sydney New York Toronto
London Auckland Johannesburg
and agencies throughout the world

First published 1998

National Library of Australia
Cataloguing-in-Publication Data

Shepherd, Janine.
Reaching for stars.

ISBN 0 091 83986 6.

1. Life Quotations, maxims, etc. I. Title.

128

Special thanks to Greg Holfeld for his wonderful illustrations.

Design by Anna Warren
Typeset by Midland Typesetters, Victoria
Printed by the australian book connection, Victoria

10 9 8 7 6 5 4 3 2 1

For Tim, Annabel, Charlotte and Angus

who have shown me that

the greatest of the three is love.

Since the publication of my two autobiographical books, *Never Tell Me Never* and *Dare to Fly*, I have been overwhelmed by the feedback I have received. My office is filled with letters and much of my time is taken replying to them. The response from readers to my books has been a great source of inspiration for me.

Many of the letters I receive are from people who have suffered an accident similar to mine and who could, therefore, relate to my story. In effect, my account of my accident was a catharsis for them as well as

4

for myself. I have laughed and I have cried at some of the stories I have read. Many of them have humbled me. Some of them have been truly heartbreaking. I have felt their pain, I have empathised with the situation in which they now find themselves, although I can offer them only words of support and love. I know they must face their situation in their own way, and in their own time. Nobody can do the healing for them.

I have been encouraged by the number of people who have written and the positive feedback I have received. Many tell how, after reading my story, they now feel able to face the challenges that lie ahead. Many have set new goals with renewed vigour, with a confidence that they once lacked. They are reaching for their own stars.

They have lived vicariously through my recovery and have gained strength from it.

Writing my story has opened up many doors for me. It launched a career on the speaking circuit and has given me the opportunity to meet so many people I would never otherwise have encountered. I can honestly say that there hasn't been one occasion when I haven't been uplifted after sharing my story with any particular group.

I always said that when I didn't enjoy speaking anymore I would stop. But as long as I feel that I have something positive to say, and that there is someone who can benefit from that, I will continue. I have been no less inspired by the people I have met as I have travelled the world.

On one occasion recently a lady told me that she had given my books to her son who was studying to be a pilot in the Australian Air Force. After reading them he passed them around his class for the others to read. That class was the first ever to have every member pass their final exams!

Another lady told me of three young men who were facing a bleak future. All of them were extremely gifted but for one reason or another they didn't see any future for themselves. Tragically, she said, one of them had been suicidal. As a last resort, she gave them my books to read. One year later, one of the boys had returned to university while the other two were now sitting their final exams to continue onto university the following year. She had written to thank me, she said, because the boy who had wanted to take his life was her son.

Many of the stories I've received have made me laugh. Recently I received a letter from a young girl who told me about her love of sport. She had medical problems which had resulted in several operations and sidelined her for most of a year. In fact, she said, she was writing her letter from her school library while all her classmates were playing sport. She had been reading my second book, *Dare to Fly*, in class when her teacher confiscated it from her. Apparently she just wasn't getting any work done. The teacher then began to read it herself and became so engrossed that she had to borrow my first book, *Never Tell Me Never* from the student to read!

Many people wrote to say they had never read a book before and mine was the first. Many wrote to say they were now facing marriage problems because they didn't speak to their husbands or wives for weeks while they were reading my books — I'm sure they were joking!

I can honestly say there can be no greater compliment for a writer to receive such feedback. It has been my honour to be able to share my story with so many people.

This book is a continuation of sharing, not only of my thoughts and reflections, but of those thoughts and sayings that continue to uplift me, particularly when times are tough. I am a great collector of all things inspirational and this is a compilation that I hope will give you some enjoyment also.

As the letters continue to come in, and as I continue to answer every one that graces my desk, I thank God for this wonderful opportunity of giving, and for each and every person that has touched my life with their equally amazing and inspiring story.

JANINE SHEPHERD
Sydney, August, 1998

If I don't manage to fly, someone else will. The spirit wants only that there be flying. As for who happens to do it, in that he has only a passing interest.

RAINER MARIA RILKE
from *Duino Elegies*

As the saying goes:

Change is constant. For many it is a gradual process, for others it may be a profound tragedy. Our ability to cope with that change defines our lives.

'One may stand still in a stream, but not in the world of man.'

As an athlete I always trained on the hills. I loved them. That is how I earned the nickname, 'Janine the Machine'. Life is full of hills and challenges. We need to do more than to take them on, we need to learn to love them, because when we can do that, there truly will be a difference in the way we face all our future challenges.

There are certain things we cannot change … other people, certain circumstances, things beyond our control. The things we can change are our attitudes, our thoughts and actions. As the well known prayer says, it is often a matter of trial and error:

God grant me the serenity

To accept the things I cannot change

The courage to change the things I can

And the wisdom to know the difference.

We are all born with differ-
ent talents and gifts. We can ignore them or
pursue them and live life to its fullest. We
need to do our best with whatever gifts we are
given, to be the best that we can be. We can
all make a unique contribution to the world.

It is in times of greatest hard-
ship that we experience the greatest personal
growth.

Sport teaches a lot of valuable lessons in life:

Don't quit.

Work as a team.

Nothing comes without hard work.

You don't always win but you can always learn something from the experience, and improve upon that performance.

Competition isn't a bad thing, if kept in perspective. It pushes us to be the best that we can be, to realise our full potential.

The marvellous richness of human experience would lose something of rewarding joy if there were no limitations to overcome.

HELEN KELLER

Your destiny can be a matter of choice

or of chance.

Courage begins when we can admit that there is no life without some pain, some frustration; no tragic accident to which we are immune. And that beyond the normal exercise of prudence we can do nothing about it.

But courage goes on to see that the triumph of life is not in pains avoided, but in joys lived completely.

Courage lies in never taking so much as a good meal or a day of good health and fair weather for granted.

It lies in being aware of our moments of happiness as sharply as our moments of pain. We need not be afraid to weep when we have cause to weep, so long as we rejoice at every cause for rejoicing.

ANONYMOUS

Setbacks in life often force us into action.

It is during the tough times that we really discover how much inner strength we have.

Remember, the tree that endures the strongest winds grows the deepest roots.

After trauma we need to allow ourselves to grieve for our loss, particularly the loss of a life once lived. Although our circumstances may have changed dramatically, there is life after an accident. It is still possible to lead a fulfilling life, to make a contribution to society.

It will certainly change you, it will definitely challenge you, but it can also lead you to the realisation of your true potential.

When placed in extreme circumstances, when faced with the need to perform at our utmost, we will surprise ourselves with our capabilities.

We all have that little bit extra, we all have a reservoir of power within.

We are all capable of extraordinary performances!

Whatever you dream of doing, start now!

Our graveyards are full of unwritten books, unfinished poems, forgotten dreams.

Who cares if you don't get published, if you don't come first?

You can say in the end, 'I did what I wanted to do.'

Tragedy does change us. It can make us bitter or better. There comes a time when we need to let go, to forgive and move on. Until we can do that, we will never reach the potential that is in us all. We will never be able to grow and to live life to its fullest.

One of my favourite authors, Richard Bach, once wrote, 'All the people, all the events in your life, are there because you have drawn them to you — what you do with them is up to you.'

Nothing in life is a coincidence. People don't turn up in our lives by chance. If we draw on these perceptions we will be sure to never miss an opportunity that presents itself.

Whenever I make the decision to do something, I make a total commitment to see it through.

Many people simply wish they could do something, but the real secret lies in taking 'action' to make it happen.

There is only one good time to start chasing your goals, and that is now!

I have never been afraid to share my dreams with others. By doing this I am proving a commitment to my goals and it gives me a great incentive to stick with it no matter what.

Dreams are extremely frag-
ile, easily broken by harsh criticism and
ridicule.

We need to tread softly with the
dreams of others, constantly uplifting them in
encouragement and support.

We have all heard people exclaim, 'Aren't they lucky!' Nobody is just lucky. So many people blame the world for their circumstances, for all their problems.

Successful people don't just grab opportunities when they arise, they go out and search for them. They create the circumstances that will lead to success.

There are always two ways to see everything. I may not be able to run a marathon with my legs, but I can run one in my heart.

When I was writing my first book, people would always ask, 'What do you do for a job?'

I would reply, 'I'm writing a book.'

'Oh really, what sort of book?' they would ask.

A little embarrassed I would say, 'Well, it's an autobiography.'

'Oh really!' came the reply. 'Who's it about?'

In our lives, pain is inevitable. Misery, however, is entirely optional.

Be the Best . . .

If you can't be a pine on top of the hill,
Be a scrub in the valley — but be the best
            little scrub
        by the side of the rill:
    Be a bush if you can't be a tree.
If you can't be a bush, be a bit of the grass,
    Doing something for somebody's sake:
If you can't be a muskie, then just be a bass,
    But the liveliest bass in the lake.

We can't all be captains,

some have to be crew,

There's something for all of us here,

There's big work and little for people to do,

And the task we must do is the near,

If you can't be a highway,

then just be a trail,

If you can't be the sun, be a star,

It isn't by size that you win or you fail,

Be the best of whatever you are!

DOUGLAS MALLOCH

Believe in yourself
and in your dreams
though impossible things may seem.
Someday, somehow,
you'll get through, to the goal
you have in view.
Mountains fall
and seas divide,
before the one
who is in their stride,
takes the hard road
day by day
sweeping obstacles away.

Believe in yourself
and in your plan,
Say not I cannot
but I can.
The prizes in life
we fail to win,
Because we doubt
the power within.

ANONYMOUS

After my accident I experienced many bouts of depression. Some days I was so low I wondered if it was worth the effort just getting out of bed. But despite the lows I knew there had to be something I could do, something I could offer this world and I couldn't give up until I had at least given it a fair go.

There are so many negative messages in the world today. We need to immerse ourselves in as much of the positive as we can. The books we read, the activities we undertake, even the people we mix with all affect our outlook on life.

Although I knew that visiting the film set of 'Never Tell Me Never' would be upsetting at times, it was something I chose to do. Seeing Claudia as myself on the day of the accident was particularly difficult, however I know it was something I needed to do. I now feel I have moved one step further in my journey of recovery.

We all need to know that we can make a difference in life. If I can make a difference, no matter how small, then all the pain and suffering has been worthwhile.

Life is a mystery to be lived,

not a problem to be solved.

ANONYMOUS

Healing doesn't come from running from

our pain.

It comes from living through the experiences.

Recovery is a painful process and takes concentrated effort.

At times it seems like an uphill battle, but with each step you become a little stronger and more able to face the next hurdle.

People always ask me about the man who was driving the car that caused my accident.

Do I feel anger for him?

It took a long time, but I have learnt to forgive and move on in my life.

Letting go of any anger has given me peace in my heart.

Besides, I don't have time to worry about him anymore, I'm too busy getting on with my life!

It is too easy after an accident, or any sort of trauma, to sit at home, feeling disconnected and isolated from the world.

It is important to get back into circulation as soon as possible, and back into community life. We all have something to offer, and becoming involved in activity of some sort helps take the focus away from our own situation and lets us realise that we are not alone in this world.

Athletes are used to using visualisation techniques to enhance performance. Research has shown that there are great benefits to mental rehearsal, in which nerve pathways are stimulated subconsciously and performance is enhanced.

I used this technique when I was learning to walk and during my rehabilitation. I used to visualise myself walking normally and then later, flying an aeroplane.

You don't need to be an athlete to use visualisation. It works for everyone.

We all find it difficult at times to deal with disappointment, we all face varying degrees of frustration in our lives. Sometimes we feel that others have let us down, in their actions or their words. I have a basket called the 'who cares' basket. Whenever I feel hurt by outside influences I just throw my worries into the basket and get on with the really important things.

When written in Chinese, the word 'crisis' is composed of two characters: one represents danger, and the other represents opportunity.

JOHN F. KENNEDY

For quite a long time after my accident, I was very self-conscious about my body. My once athletic, powerful physique was gone and I was left with a rather pathetic image that I resented.

I felt robbed of my self, my self-esteem was depleted. But I now feel grateful for what this new body has allowed me to achieve, and I realise strength cannot be measured by physique but by character.

Knowing Uncle Darryl taught me many things in life.

So many of us miss the opportunity to tell others just how much they mean to us. I made that mistake once, but I now know I will never let that happen again.

My recovery was ten percent physical and ninety percent mental.

The battle over our minds is the greatest of all.

Even though I never saw the faces of the other patients in the spinal ward and didn't know what they looked like, we all developed deep friendships with each other. It really was a unique situation.

Sometimes we make judgements on first appearances without ever really getting to know the person within.

In Norman Cousin's book, *Anatomy of an Illness*, he details how he recovered from a life-threatening disease through the medicine of laughter.

Laughter releases endorphins, the body's natural opiate, which promotes a sense of well-being and overall good health.

When I was in hospital, my sister Kelley supplied me with comedy videos which not only provided light relief from my condition but offered relaxation and pain relief.

We cannot overestimate the healing power of laughter — that is the reason I married an Irishman!

A friend of mine gave me this. It says it all.

Why Worry?

There are only two things to worry about — either you are well or you are sick. If you are well, then there is nothing to worry about. But if you are sick, there are two things to worry about. Either you will get well or you will die. If you get well, there is nothing to worry about. If you die there are only two things to worry about — either you will go to heaven or hell. If you go to heaven, there is nothing to worry about. But if you go to hell, you'll be so darn busy shaking hands with friends, you won't have time to worry!

I t is too easy to feel that we are the only ones suffering.

The truth is that all of us have our own personal degrees of pain, our own trials to deal with.

Nobody can cope alone.

The burden is eased when we share our pain with others and let them into our lives.

I have taken many risks in my life. Learning to fly was a great risk. I knew nothing about flying, I knew no-one who could fly. I couldn't even walk — who was I kidding!

I even had my doubts that what I was doing was unrealistic. I was really stepping out of my comfort zone. But despite this I had to go anyway.

I pushed the fear and doubts to the back of my mind and filled my thoughts with images of what I wanted to see.

If we didn't take any risks in life, we wouldn't experience anything new.

How boring life would be!

Recovery from trauma can be an overwhelming process.

Learning to fly could have seemed too gargantuan a task — I didn't even know if I would be able to pass a pilot's medical! But I just concentrated on the next lesson, I didn't look too far ahead, because that would have been too daunting.

It's true: 'Inch by Inch, it's a cinch!'

In flying, we use the formula:
ATTITUDE + POWER = PERFORMANCE. In
an aircraft, the 'attitude' is the relationship of
the nose of the aircraft to the horizon, the
power is generated from the engine, and the
performance is the capability of the aircraft.

The pilot is in direct control of
the 'attitude' of the aircraft via the control
stick — just a small adjustment can alter its
flight path through the air. Just like the
aircraft, our attitude controls our flight path
through life, and we can easily adjust it by
altering the thoughts that go through our
heads.

Our power comes from pure hard work. Nothing was ever achieved without it. Nobody was going to walk for me; I had to work at it. I had to do it myself. And the same goes for my flying. Sure, it was a struggle at times, but the rewards are in the life I now lead.

If we have the right attitude, the 'Never Tell Me Never' and the 'Dare to Fly' attitude, and we work as hard as we can, then we will perform — we will achieve our goals.

Attitude + Power = Performance is a mathematical formula that works in our flying and in our lives!

No matter how well we plan a flight, we can never totally predict the elements we might encounter en route. Wind, rain, storms, and other variables all affect our track and we need to make the necessary adjustments to our heading along the way to stay on track.

Sometimes our original destination is thwarted and we need to plan for an alternative — another landing place.

We can rigidly plan our future but sometimes we come across 'storms' in our lives. Sometimes we can make small adjustments and stay on track for the goals we have set ourselves.

But other times we need to make the decision to change our original path and head off in search of a new destination.

The greatest barrier to success is fear.

Take solace in knowing that we all experience it — we all fear certain things: fear of falling, fear of failure, even fear of flying!

But courage comes from not letting our fear disable us from achieving the things we dream of doing. It isn't the absence of fear but the mastery of it that makes the difference.

The best way to conquer fear is to go out and do the thing you fear most. In doing that we gain the confidence to tackle the next fear and overcome the next obstacle that stands in our way.

Flying has given me so much, has taught me so many things. It helped me get back on my feet, literally and figuratively. It was the ultimate sense of freedom, particularly after the spinal ward.

When I decided to learn aerobatics, there were always questions over whether I would be able to control the aeroplane with the lack of strength in my legs. But my philosophy has always been, if you never have a go, you never, never know!

One of the most difficult aspects of my accident was the loss of control. No matter how hard I tried, I had to acknowledge that my injuries were permanent and that I would have to learn to live with them.

When I learnt to fly, I discovered the ultimate freedom. It was just me and the machine and I was in control.

That did wonders for my self-esteem.

I have heard it said that to be happy we all need something to love, something to do, and something to hope for.

Nobody can tell you what heights you can soar to. Not even you will know until you spread your wings.

Flying on instruments is rewarding and challenging, but for me the great joy in flying is looking outside at the vast landscape and beauty below.

In life it is important to take time to look outside and appreciate the wonderful gifts of nature that surround us.

To be successful at anything in life, I believe you must have the three D's.

Desire: you have to be hungry

Dedication: you must be committed to the task

Determination: you need that Never-give-up attitude.

Whenever I give a talk, there is always someone who comes up to me afterwards and says, 'I've always wanted to fly'. I ask, 'Why don't you then?'

'Oh, you know', comes the answer. 'I'm too old, it's too late, not enough money...'

The excuses are neverending.

Whatever you want to do in life, whether it be flying, bungy jumping, or riding a Harley to Ayres Rock, I say, just do it!

You may not be as fortunate as me — you may not get a second chance!

No matter where we are in life, we will all come across tough times. We need to remember that we are all connected in some way, and whenever possible we need to reach out and lend a helping hand to those in need.

Just the simple words, 'Can I help?' can make a world of difference to another.

When I decided to learn to fly I was still unable to walk. I knew it would be difficult staying focused on my goal, so I kept a daily diary of my physical progress. In my old training diary I would record everything from the hours of sleep I had, to my pulse rate to how many repetitions of exercises I had managed. Although the progress was extremely slow, I was able to see that I was getting stronger every day, and this was my incentive to keep pushing.

In an aeroplane we have an instrument called the 'turn and balance co-ordinator'. To maintain smooth and balanced flight we need to use the rudder pedals to keep the balance ball in the centre, and thus keep the aircraft on track. We can easily let our lives get 'out of balance' — sometimes we focus too much attention on some areas and forget other equally important aspects. We all need to lead balanced lives.

Fear can be paralysing.

By succumbing to fear we fail to take the steps needed for personal growth and fulfilment.

Fear is natural. Accepting it and living with it is the first step to overcoming it.

Positive thinking really does work.

Whenever I am faced with a challenging situation, when it is difficult to see the light at the end of the tunnel, I believe and know that things will work out. I can see the possibilities as if they have already happened.

Our thoughts create reality.

P.S. Negative thinking works just as effectively. It's just not what I'm interested in!

I wonder how many new things we would attempt if the possibility of failure wasn't a part of the equation?

It's no use having a destination, if you
can't enjoy the journey.

The great secret to success is to know what you want, then truly *believe* that you can achieve it.

There is no hill too steep that it can't be climbed, no problem too difficult that it can't be solved. Creativity and persistence go a long way to solving any problem.

I believe in the power of affir-mations.

Whenever I face difficult times I always remind myself, 'I will handle it'... and I always do.

A successful person is not the one who has never tasted failure, but the one who continues to move forward despite the obstacles.

Your Dream

Your dreams may be big, may be wild,
may be grand,
It's probably something only
you understand.
But as long as you hold it close to your heart
You and your dream will not be apart.

Maybe no one has achieved it before
But that only makes it more exciting for sure
There will be many doubters along the way,
Do not be disheartened by the things
they will say.

There will always be someone who says
you can't do it,
So you must rely on yourself to get
through it.
Just put your head down and go for
your goal,
Put everything into it, your heart and
your soul

If you do these things it will not be long —
Before you have proven your doubters
were wrong.

LUCY MCMAHON

(Lucy wrote this poem and sent it to me with the
words ... Dedicated to 'Janine the Machine!')

When we are feeling the weight of the world on our shoulders, we don't have to look very far to find someone who is worse off than ourselves. Remember to always 'count your blessings' — it helps put things back in perspective.

Our challenge in life is to do the best we can, with what we have, for as long as we are able.

Nothing in the world can take the place of persistence. Talent will not; nothing is more common that unsuccessful men with talent. Genius will not; unrewarded genius is almost a proverb. Education alone will not; the world is full of educated derelicts. Persistence and determination alone are omnipotent.

CALVIN COOLIDGE

Treat every child like a potential genius. It is our responsibility as adults to nurture their ability, to give them every opportunity to reach greatness.

We can become too rigid in our ways. Often we can be heading for our goals, when something happens to force us to change track.

We can fight it, but it will ultimately lead to frustration. Or we can accept the circumstances, just as we accept the inevitable change in weather patterns when we are flying. We need to adjust our instruments, replot our flight path and continue in the other direction.

Your attitude, not aptitude, determines
your altitude.

ANONYMOUS

Sometimes I think that in today's hectic

pace we are all so busy *doing*

and not just *being.*

I have found that people who have a strong personal philosophy in life usually cope far better in times of hardship.

My faith has given me strength in times of despair. I have always believed that God has been with me every step of the way, guiding me, protecting me, loving me. This has given me a great sense of peace and acceptance in my life.

Someone once said, Life is God's gift to you, and the way you live it is your gift to God.

We were born with incredible determination. As babies we all had that 'never give up' attitude. Watching my children learn to walk, I could appreciate just how difficult a task it was. I know what it was like to learn all over again. They stumble, they fall, but they just keep getting up. They never give up. There really is a lesson to be learnt from that.

People always ask me 'is it difficult to write a book?' I tell them yes and no. The writing wasn't the hard part — when you have a passion to do something it is easy. The difficult part was having to write with my daughter sitting on my lap!

I needed to write my story because I didn't want the memory of what I had been through to disappear. Even though some of the past experiences are painful to recollect, they are part of the connection with myself. To deny them is to deny the life I have lived.

For a long time it seemed to me that life was about to begin — real life. But there was always some obstacle in the way, something to be got through first, some unfinished business, time to be served, a debt to be paid. Then life would begin. At last it dawned on me that these obstacles were my life.

ALFRED D'SOUZA

When I first met Tim, I was somewhat hesitant to share my 'problems' with him. There were some very personal issues I had to deal with. I felt sure he wouldn't want to put up with someone who is definitely 'high maintenance'.

I remember asking one day, 'Wouldn't you rather be with someone who is normal?'

He replied, 'Normal? How boring!'

He always has a way of making me feel special, even in his own 'funny' way.

No Matter What Else

No matter what else you're doing,
From cradle days through to the end,
You're writing your life's secret story,
Each night sees another page penned.
Each month ends a thirty-day chapter,
Each year the end of a part,
And never an act is mis-stated
Not even a wish of the heart.
Each morn when you wake the book opens,
Revealing a page clean and white,
What words and what thoughts and what doings
Will cover its surface at night?

God leaves that to you, you're the writer

And never a word will grow dim

Until you'll write the word 'finished'

And give your life's book back to him.

(This was sent to me from Carli Triffit. Her grandad used to recite this to her ... each time a little differently!)

My greatest achievement has been having my children. It has undoubtedly been my greatest challenge, and my greatest joy. I have a quote pinned on my fridge that says it all:

A child will make love stronger

Days shorter

Nights longer

Pay packets emptier

Homes happier

Clothes shabbier

The past forgotten

And the future worth living.

Never is a word I don't accept!

I was never meant to live, walk again or ever have children, let alone ever lead a normal life. The only limits we face are the ones we construct ourselves.

So often we let the trivial things in life upset us. It really isn't until something profound happens in our lives that we put things in perspective and realise how insignificant most of our worries really are.

Life seems to be happening too quickly these days. As a parent I feel the pressure to race around with my children participating in every activity on offer.

I relish the days when we can come home from school and do absolutely nothing! There is plenty of time to rush around, but those days at home will be gone all too quickly.

No matter what happens in life, I always look for the meaning behind it. I can learn from every situation — nothing happens in vain. Instead of a random path through life, I have found a logical progression which has given my life a sense of purpose.

In science there is a phenomenon known as the Butterfly Principle. If a butterfly beats its wings today in Peking, the effect can transform storm systems next month in New York. A small input creates a large effect.

It doesn't take much in our lives to make a huge difference to the lives of others, even by the simplest of deeds.

I t isn't the meaning of life that's important,
it's the meaning *in* life.

We need to ask ourselves constantly, If everyone in the world was doing what I am doing, would the world be a better place?

If the answer is yes, you know you must be doing something right.

Throughout my accident and recovery, I had incredible support from my family and friends. Their love sustained me, particularly during the most difficult times.

There is great healing power in love.

All too often we let our situation overwhelm us. We can too easily feel the weight of the world on our shoulders. We lose perspective. Each night when I tuck my children into bed, and kiss them goodnight, my problems seem insignificant.

Nothing could be that important!

People often call me a 'motivational' speaker. I don't like that expression. I prefer to use the word 'inspirational'.

We can inspire another person with our lives, but we can't motivate them. Motivation is something that must come from within.

My life is getting more and more hectic. I remind myself constantly that I need to slow down, take on less commitments and just spend time with my family doing ordinary things.

With so much talk about 'quality' time, it is important to remember that nothing can replace 'quantity' time.

Instead of wondering, *what if?* I prefer to think about, *what is*. We need to work with the gifts we have and make the most out of every situation.

Victor Frankl once wrote, 'He who has a why to live can bear with almost any how.'

When we can find some purpose in our suffering, we are given a renewed strength to keep going even during the most difficult times.

I am always amazed when people ask new mothers, 'So when are you going back to work?' So often our worth is measured by the work we do outside the home. The real work however is that which is done around the kitchen table. There is no job more important, or more fulfilling, than raising a family or being part of one.

Somebody once said,

The world we leave to our children, depends

on the children we leave to our world.

I have often been asked about hope. Shouldn't we avoid giving people false hope? Well, I say, maybe that is better than no hope at all, because when you have no hope, you have nothing to live for. Despite changing circumstances, there is always the hope to lead a fulfilling life, of being able to contribute in a positive way to life and to society.

Great marriages don't just happen. They take energy, patience, dedication, determination, commitment and a shared vision. They require sacrifice and a selfless attitude.

But anything worth having is worth the effort.

It is absolutely necessary to have goals in life. Unfortunately, many of us get them mixed up. The most important goals are those relating to family — that is where real fulfilment comes from. As the saying goes, Nobody says on their deathbed, 'Gee, I wish I'd spent more time at the office'!

We all have the potential to do much more than we are doing now. When I was in hospital all I wanted to do was to walk, when I could walk all I wanted to do was to fly, and when I could fly all I wanted to do was to fly an FA-18 fighter jet ... and I have done that too!

Anything is possible!

I have been fortunate to have been able to share my story with so many others. I am always amazed, and humbled by the feedback I have received. I believe there is a great amount of hope in knowing that others have endured equally traumatic circumstances and have beaten the odds.

When I look back on my recovery, I know I came to a point when I was heading for a crash landing. When I saw that aircraft above, I knew what I had to do. I had to adjust my attitude, and apply the power necessary to get me back into life. I knew I couldn't change what had happened to me, but I could change my attitude towards those things. It's not what you have that counts, it's how you use what you have.

The greatest gift we can give our children is an optimistic outlook on life. With that we have given them the tools to effectively cope with any of life's challenges.

You can never really expect anything of this life for you will only be led to disappointments. Remember, it is actually this life that is expecting something of you!

Life is a juxtaposition. It isn't painful and horrible or joyful and wonderful ... it is both.

The greatest service in life is the service to humanity. You can have anything you want, go anywhere you want in life, as long as you help as many others along the way.

Sometimes life's greatest problems turn out to be life's greatest blessings.

As much as I would have loved to have competed at the Olympics, nothing could ever compare with holding my newborn babe in my arms, not even a Gold Medal!

There is vitality, a life force, an energy, a quickening, which is translated through you into action.

And because there is only one you in all time, this expression is unique and if you block it, it will never exist through any other medium and the world will not have it.

MARTHA GRAHAM

A friend gave me a copy of the following letter written by a father to his grown-up daughter. Its message is priceless.

My hands were busy through the day
I didn't have much time to play
The little games you asked me to
I didn't have much time for you

I'd work hard all day to provide things
for you
But when you'd bring your picture-book
And ask me please to share your fun
I'd say — a little later — my darling

I'd tuck you in all safe at night
And hear your prayers — turn out the light
Then tip toe softly to the door
I wish I'd stayed a minute more

For life is short and the years rush past

A little child grows up so fast

No longer are they at your side

Their precious secrets to confide

The picture books are put away

There are no children's games to play

No goodnight kiss — no prayers to hear

That all belongs to yesteryear

My hands once busy — now lie still

The days are long and hard to fill

How I long to go back and do

The little things you asked me to

Even allowing for all the pressures on couples today it's important to remember that life is what's passing us by while we're planning for the future.

If I had my Life to live over again

If I had my life to live over, I'd dare to make
more mistakes next time.
I'd relax. I'd limber up. I would be sillier
than I have this time.
I would take fewer things seriously.
I would take more chances.
I would take more trips.
I would climb more mountains
and swim more rivers.
I would eat more ice cream and less beans.
I would perhaps have more actual troubles,
but I'd have fewer imaginary ones.

You see. I am one of those people who live sensibly and sanely, hour after hour, day after day. Oh, I've had my moments, and if I had it to do over again, I'd have more of them. In fact, I'd try to have nothing else. Just moments, one after another, instead of living so many years ahead of each day.

I've been one of those persons who never goes anywhere without a thermometer, a hot water bottle, a raincoat and a parachute. If I had my life to live over, I would start barefoot earlier in the spring and I would stay that way later in the fall. I would go to more dances. I would ride more merry-go-rounds. I would pick more daisies.

BY NADINE STAIR, 85 YEARS OLD
LOUISVILLE, KENTUCKY

I hope my children
look back on today
and see parents
who had time to play.
There will be years
for cleaning and cooking,
but children grow up
while we are not looking.
Dusting and scrubbing
can wait till tomorrow,
for babies grow fast,
we learn to our sorrow.
So quiet down cobwebs
and dust go to sleep.
I'm rocking my baby
and babies don't keep.

ANONYMOUS

Rilke *never* said I give you the answers. He said love the questions and perhaps you'll live your way into the answers.

RAINER MARIA RILKE
Introduction from *Duino Elegies*

As I compiled my thoughts and reflections for this collection I once again relived many of the emotions that I have been through since my accident. Once again it has given me the opportunity to move forward in my journey and my recovery.

Many times I wondered about the value of what I have been through. Indeed, many people ask me: 'If you could pass on one piece of advice, one insight, what would it be?'

There have been so many lessons, so many subplots, how could I possibly put it down to one factor? It's not that simple.

I have undergone so many changes since the accident, and indeed, I still do. Where would I start? What is most relevant, most succinct lesson I learned during this time?

Is it that life is filled with heartache, yet despite this there are moments of pure joy? Is it about perseverance, or courage? Or is it about acceptance — of my situation? Of my physical self? Of self-love?

Is it about the determination to keep going, of never giving up despite the overwhelming factors against us? Of knowing you have given it your best and you have beaten the odds?

Or is it about always maintaining hope, for now and the future?

Or about friendship, old and new?Perhaps it's about the ability to stay positive when everything around you seems negative. Is it attitude?

Or is it learning to trust again? In life, and circumstances around us? In God? In learning to take risks? In chancing losing, but having a go anyway.

Or is it in learning to laugh again — in seeing the humour in the life around you?

Or learning to love again? In baring your soul to another?

For a long time after my accident I had desperately searched for some tangible meaning behind everything, wanting to find the missing piece of the jigsaw, the reason all this had happened. I searched high and low for answers, convinced that if I found them everything would fall into place. It became my obsession.

But as the years passed, I found myself relaxing. The need to know was gradually replaced with a sense of acceptance and peace. I was so busy living life that I had forgotten about the questions. They didn't seem important anymore. I was living the questions.

In attempting to simplify my journey for this book I realised that the answer to my question was in fact, the sum of my experiences. There was no one lesson to be learnt, I discovered, for life itself is the lesson. Reaching the top of the mountain is not nearly as important as the climb to the top.It hasn't been easy, but then anything in life worth having is worth hurting for.

The struggles are ongoing, but life's trials refine us. They build character and strength. They shape our lives. They help us to see what is really important in life. They give us perspective.

It has taken a long time to reach this realisation but it has been a turning point in my life. My accident has taught me more about life and more about myself than any other single experience I could have wished for.

It has changed me. It has softened my heart. I know I am a better person for it.

In life as our circumstances change, so do our priorities. My focus has shifted greatly over the years.

I have learned to love, to care, to serve.

I now understand that the greatest healing force on earth is unconditional love. As Virgil says, *love conquers all*. There remains no doubt in my mind that through the simple act of love, all things are possible.

To love and to be loved is the greatest blessing in life.

The Bible speaks highly of the three greatest attributes: *And now these three remain; Faith, Hope and Love, but the greatest of these is Love.*

My greatest blessing in life has been my wonderful husband Tim and our three adored children. They have truly completed my life, they are my hope for the future. Their love has sustained me. They have taught me so much about myself and what I have endured. They have taught me to look outwards rather than inwards. They have shown me that I lack nothing, for in them I have everything.

Love gives naught but itself and takes naught but from itself.

Love possesses not nor would it be possessed;

For love is sufficient unto love.

KAHLIL GIBRAN